SIN-FULL & SHAME-LESS

Natalie Stack

AuthorHouse™
1663 Liberty Drive
Bloomington, IN 47403
www.authorhouse.com
Phone: 1 (800) 839-8640

Published by AuthorHouse 10/27/2018

ISBN: 978-1-5462-6597-9 (sc)
ISBN: 978-1-5462-6598-6 (e)

Library of Congress Control Number: 2018912928

Print information available on the last page.

Any people depicted in stock imagery provided by Getty Images are models, and such images are being used for illustrative purposes only. Certain stock imagery © Getty Images.

This book is printed on acid-free paper.

authorHOUSE®

Stuff You Need to Know

When it comes to building something beautiful, you have to have the right tools. The first thing you need in baking, is pride. Pride in the taste, pride in it looking yummy and pride in yourself.

You'll see two prominent ingredients in here, Chocolate and Lemon. I don't have a monumental reason why, it's just my opinion that they make the best **Sin-full** desserts. So my suggestion is, if chocolate is your nirvana, go to a Chocolateier, like Bernard Callebaut's and get a brick, or buy good chocolate in bulk. You'll use it, and in the long run, far cheaper than buying bags of chocolate chips. As you'll see, I do not mention any particular chocolate. That's because it's all about preference. I love dark chocolate, I find the bitterness of it, is like a good cup of coffee to me. However, there isn't a whole lot of us out there, so it's 100% up to you which one sings to you, milk, white, orange flavored or dark.

The equipment is next, nothing needs to cost a lot of money unless you have it and want to spend it. But anyone can bake with a cake pan, cookie sheet and a whisk if you don't have anything more, but desire. Just one little thing that you'll need to purchase if you don't have one, a scale. There aren't a lot of recipes in this wee book that needs a scale, but a couple that just didn't work for me by using cups, so I turned to grams and happy face for me! You can get them most places that sells baking pans and such, in a wide range of prices, so pick the one that gives you a happy face.

You want to make a light, fluffy, moist cake, cupcake or muffin, so you should sift your dry ingredients. It's not a punishable offense If you don't, but it really lightens up the batter by incorporating air. Sift at least once, but there isn't a magic number to go by, I generally sift three times and that's enough to lighten things up. Cake and pastry flour, are your best friend. For every ½ cup of All Purpose Flour, you need to weigh **74** grams of C&P. Again, it's not life or death, but it's a light flour to begin with. Air. Air is a natural leavening, which means it helps it rise. The more air you incorporate into your batters, the better result. Except muffins, no to beating a muffin batter too long, it has the opposite effect. They become hockey pucks. But with cakes, that's the reason why we beat the batter for 3-5 minutes and why it ends up lighter in color, that's the air. Also, you'll see "eggs separated" which means you'll be folding in the whipped egg whites, again for fluffy, airy cakes. If it doesn't state that, by all means separate your eggs, whip and fold the whites in the last stage before pouring into pan.

We covered fluffy, now lets chat about moist. Most recipes call for vegetable oil or butter, reason being is because you need the fat for the "moist" part. I'm going to give you a new one, **Grape Seed Oil**. It has a ton of uses that google can clear up for you, but I'll tell you why I use Grape Seed Oil. No flavour. It still has the fat content, but it has more of the "good" fat, plus it's very high in Omega 3, which makes me feel better about eating that chocolate cake. I want my cakes to taste like the flavour I put into the batter, not the oil that moistens it.

Save, time double the recipe. I've been as crazy as times 4, it'll work out just as good.

The last thing you need to know is, baking should be fun. Even when you make mistakes, and trust me, you'll make them, have FUN! Crank your music, sing into your spatula, dance around the broken egg on the flour, because if you're baking.......IT'S A DELICOUSLY GOOD DAY!

I wrote this cookbook for two reasons, first one being when I was working at a resort doing what I love, baking. I was experimenting with flavor combos on a daily basis for my desserts & handheld delights, but I needed a "tester." I found willing participants easily enough, but the one friend that consistently was eager to try my crazy, sometimes weird mash ups, was Olivia . Everyday she would come from her duties at the resort to meet up with me for a snack & chat, to offer her take on the days yumminess. I found myself disappointed when her work prevented her from making our break, to the point that I would find her, just to see if todays offering was good enough to offer to the public.

Olivia mentioned more than once that she wishes she could do this, that she could cook or bake something delicious. "I am the worst cook EVER, & my baking is terrible" We laughed about it, & I told her, you only have to try, & it was forgotten until one beautiful winter day in February, she came running up to me, with excitement radiating from her. " I did it! I cooked something & it wasn't horrible! I mean, it wasn't perfect, but it was GOOD!" I could see the pride, the absolute joy on her face because she did it, because she stepped out of her comfort zone & accomplished something she thought she was incapable of doing.

That's when I knew that she isn't alone in the world & perhaps they too would like to learn how to bake, how to discover they might not be as bad at it as they think. So I knew I could help with a very easy way to make something from scratch, to create old tried & true recipes easier to follow. To have that pride on their face.

The second reason to write this book was the idea to take rich desserts loaded with fat & sugar, to a trimmer, more health conscience approach that came from my body building son in-law Kyle. Who can't resist a sweet treat, but doesn't want the extra pounds, or the guilt for indulging. It was his suggestion for a high carb, low fat dessert. He too isn't alone in this world in believing that desserts are essential as keeping your body healthy, but without the guilt or the feeling of missing out.

So I wrote this cookbook for the Olivia Miltons & Kyle Northcotts of the world, for healthy individuals that like to eat desserts without Shame and for the "Worst cooks ever" to becoming Bakers.

Contents

Sin-full 1

   Chocolate Lava Cake 3

   Lemon Ricotta Torte 4

   White Cake 5

   Chocolate Cake 6

   Lemon Poppy Seed Pound Cake 7

   Chocolate Mousse No Bake Cheesecake .8

   Chunky Mini Cakes 10

   Double Chocolate Chunk Cookies 11

   Salty & Sweet Squirrel Cookies 13

   Coconut Chunk Cookies 15

Shame- less 17

   Just Try It Brownies 18

   Bran Mini Cakes 19

   Raspberry Swirly Cheesecake 20

   Oat & Raisin Cookies 21

   Pumpkin Mini Cakes 22

   Apple Crunch Cookies 23

   Monkey Mini Cakes 24

   White Chocolate & Cranberry Cookies 25

   Raspberry Lemon Mini Cakes 26

This & That 27

   Buttercream Frosting 28

   Crust of Sir Graham 29

   Lemon Curd 30

   Ganache 31

   Truffles 33

   Granola Bars 34

   Egg – Less 36

   Pumpkin Spice 37

   Caramel 38

   Thick Caramel 39

SIN-FULL

CHOCOLATE LAVA CAKE

40 grams chocolate of your choice. Chips, bar, or a chunk from your local chocolate shop
½ cup butter

1 cup powdered sugar
2 eggs plus 2 egg yolks room temp
6 tblsps flour
4 small or 2 large ramekins

Preheat oven to 425 degrees - spray or grease with butter the ramekins and place on a cookie sheet

Melt chocolate and butter in microwave 1 minute, stir until smooth. Add powdered sugar, again until smooth. Add eggs and beat for 1 minute, add flour and beat for an additional 1 minute. Spoon into ramekins ¾ full and bake **12-13 minutes.** Remove from oven and gently run your knife around the edges, place your serving plate on top of cake and flip, remove ramekin. Hopefully it comes out whole, but if not, better luck next time? It's still delicious.

- *To make this a truly sinful and an eye catching dessert……before you make your Lava Cake….take 1 ½ cups of raspberries, or berries of your choice add them to a small saucepan with 2 tblsps of water and cook down on low heat until it becomes a chunky sauce, approx. 5 minutes. This you spoon over the cake before serving, with a scoop of vanilla ice cream…… genius.*

- *OR cook down (reduce) 2 cups of Orange Juice until it thickens, about 5 mins, for your sauce*

LEMON RICOTTA TORTE

Or a fancy name for skinny cake. This is a perfect summer dessert because it's a light piece of sunshine.

¾ cup butter
¾ cup sugar
4 lemons zested and juiced – set aside
2 tblsps of zest for garnish
3 egg yolks
3 egg whites whipped until firm peaks
1 cup ricotta

½ cup flour
2 tsp baking powder
¼ tsp salt
Lemon curd – see recipe in "**This and That"**
A cup of whipped cream

Preheat oven at 320 degrees, grease and line bottom of torte pan with parchment, if you don't have a Fluted Torte Pan, a round cake pan will do as nicely. Be aware that batter will only fill 1/3 of the regular cake pan.

Have your egg whites whipped to a stiff peak and lemons zested and juiced, set aside. Cream butter and sugar, add lemon, egg yolks and ricotta, beat until smooth. In a separate bowl, combine flour, baking powder and salt. Gradually add to lemon mixture until smooth, fold in egg whites then pour into prepared pan and bake for **30 minutes** or until toothpick inserted in the middle comes out clean.

- *Slice torte into 10 pieces*
- *If you want to get really fancy, decorate the bottom of your serving plate with a smear of whipped cream*
- *Spoon a small amount of lemon curd, and a dollop of whipped cream on top of torte and sprinkle lemon zest*

WHITE CAKE

½ cup butter

1 cup sugar

2 eggs

1/3 cup veg oil

2 tsp vanilla extract

1 ½ cup flour

2 tsp baking powder

¼ tsp salt

½ cup milk

Preheat oven to 350 degrees, grease and flour 2 round cake pans, a rectangle pan, or bundt pan

Cream butter and sugar until smooth and light in color (approx. 2 mins) add eggs, veg oil and vanilla, beat for 3 minutes. In a separate bowl mix flour, baking powder and salt, gradually add to butter sugar mixture, alternating with milk (approx. 3 mins) until smooth. Pour into prepared pan(s) and **bake 20 to 30 minutes**, or until toothpick inserted in the center comes out clean. Cool completely before removing from pans and/or frosting.

- *This is the perfect stepping stone cake, it's light and delicious on its own topped with berries and whip cream.*

- *I recommend adding a ½ cup of white chocolate after the batter is mixed before pouring into your pan. For an added treat frost with a flavoured buttercream.*

- *This can be a lovely lemon cake by adding 1 tsp of lemon exract, baked in two round pans, with a spread of lemon curd in between the layers, frost with a vanilla buttercream, which you can find in "**This & That"** for both.*

- *A truly sinful way to enjoy this simple cake is serving it with a drizzle of your favourite liqueur alone or topped with chocolate sauce and ice cream.*

CHOCOLATE CAKE

1/3 cup vegetable oil
1 cup sugar
2 eggs
1 cup milk
½ cup applesauce
2 tsp vanilla extract

1 ¾ cup flour
2/3 cup cocoa
1 ½ tsp baking powder
1 ½ tsp baking soda
1 cup boiling water

Preheat oven to 350 degrees, grease and flour 2 round cake pans, a rectangle or bundt pan

Cream oil and sugar, add egg, milk, applesauce, and extract, beat for 3 minutes. In a separate bowl combine flour, cocoa, baking powder, soda and salt. Slowly add to oil and sugar mixture, alternating with boiling water. Pour into prepared pan(s) and bake **20 to 30 minutes** or until a toothpick inserted in the center comes out clean. Cool completely before removing and/or frosting.

- *To make this a double chocolate cake add ½ cup of chocolate, white or dark before pouring into your pan.*
- *OR for a truly decadent Sin-full cake, make it a triple chocolate by frosting the cake with chocolate buttercream*
- *Instead of vanilla extract, shake it up with a different flavor. such as orange*

LEMON POPPY SEED POUND CAKE

My grandmother would have served this cake with tea to "company." Me? I like any hand held treat to eat on the way to the gym…..umm, yeah no, it's a snack that given a chance turns into a BIG snack, it's that delicious

675 grams butter
675 g sugar
6 eggs
3 lemons, juice and zest, ½ tblsp of zest for garnish

3 tblsp poppyseed
675 g flour
6 tsp baking powder
¼ tsp salt

Preheat oven to 350 degrees, grease and flour a loaf pan

Cream butter and sugar, add eggs, lemon juice and zest. In a separate bowl, combine poppyseed, flour, baking powder and salt. Slowly add to butter sugar mixture until combined, then pour into prepared pan and bake **45-50 minutes** or until a toothpick inserted in the center comes out clean

- *Too get fancy, remove cooled cake from pan and drizzle with ½ tblsp of lemon juice combined with a ¼ cup of powdered sugar. If too thick to drizzle add water ¼ tsp at a time until you have a smooth glaze*

- *To make this cake a parfait, cut cake into cubes and layer in a nice glass (drink martinis? Perfect) with berries and whipped cream*

CHOCOLATE MOUSSE NO BAKE CHEESECAKE

This dessert is beyond chocolate goodness that is simple and takes no time to prepare. It looks and tastes decadent without you breaking a sweat to make, as you don't need to turn on your oven.

1 1/3 cup chocolate cookie crumbs
1/3 cup butter melted
2 cups whipped cream, 1 cup for topping
½ cup powdered sugar

10 oz cream cheese, room temperature
¼ cup plain yogurt
1 tsp of vanilla
8 oz semi – sweet chocolate, melted and slightly cooled

Line 8x8 pan with parchment paper

Mix the cookie crumbs with the melted butter and press firmly onto the bottom of your pan, refrigerate while preparing the rest of the yummy goodness

Whip the cream and slowly add the powdered sugar until you have formed stiff peaks, set aside

In a separate bowl, beat cream cheese, yogurt and vanilla until smooth, then slowly add the melted chocolate. When smooth, fold in the whipped cream until fully incorporated. Pour into prepared pan, top with remaining cream, sprinkle choc shavings and chill for a minimum of **4 hours.**

- *To make the chocolate shavings, use your vegetable peeler to "shave" a piece of chocolate. You used chips? Can you imagine trying to shave them? Haha, just sprinkle on top*

- *Want to look like a Rock Star? Use a flavoured chocolate! Just imagine biting into a Coconut Chocolate Cheesecake? Or Orange? Whatever flavour makes you happy, try it, guaranteed the crowd goes wild!*

- *How about white chocolate? Surprise!*

CHUNKY MINI CAKES

This is chocolate with a little cake.

112 gr vegetable oil
245 gr plain yogurt
122.5 gr milk
1 egg
201 gr sugar

256 gr flour
1 ½ tsp baking soda
160 gr chocolate, chopped into chunks

Preheat oven to 400 degrees and line 12 muffin cups with your pretty liners.

Whisk all the wet ingredients until frothy, set aside. In a separate bowl mix the dry ingredients including your chunky chocolate. Once thoroughly combined add to the wet bowl all at once. Just mix until combined and using a 6oz ice cream scoop fill cups 2/3 full. If the scoop doesn't say the size, it's the big one. Bake **20 minutes.**

- *This recipe begs to be doubled, or you'll be making them again tomorrow, just saying*
- *Yep you guessed it, to make this a double chunky diet cheater choice add **64 gr** cocoa with the dry ingredients*
- *The best tip for this oh so yummy muffin, is cool at least 20 minutes before eating, it's hard to resist, but it needs to set a bit or you have a crumbly chocolate mess on your floor*

DOUBLE CHOCOLATE CHUNK COOKIES

I'm cutting right to the chase here, no need to see the footnotes first to decide how much chocolate, because you'll add the extra chocolate anyway, right? I usually double or triple this recipe because I like a lot of cookies, for the kids, friends or just to horde for my late night snacking.

1 cup butter	2/3 cup cocoa
1 cup sugar	¾ tsp baking soda
2 eggs	¼ tsp salt
2 tsp vanilla	2 cups chocolate chunks, chips if you
2 cups flour	forgot to get the good stuff

Preheat oven to 350 degrees

Cream butter and sugar until the color changes to a light yellow, approx. 2 mins. Beat in eggs and vanilla until combined and fluffy. Sift all the dry ingredients together and slowly add to the wet until combined, add your chunks and beat until not a piece of chocolate is left in the bottom of the bowl. With a 6oz ice cream scoop, drop onto your cookie sheet with room in between as the spread a little and press down until they are even all around. Bake **12 mins for large cookies, medium 10 mins, small 8 mins.** If you don't trust yourself that they are baked enough, trust **ME.** Cool 15 mins before sampling.

- *To make a nice round, even cookie, use a cookie ring and depending on size of ring, you might need 2 scoops of dough. No matter the size of the ring, press the cookie until it's approx. 1 inch thick*

- *When completely cooled, make a sandwich with softened vanilla ice cream, wrap individually and freeze*

- *If you haven't gotten enough chocolate, dip your cookie or sandwich in melted chocolate. Depending how much of the cookie you dip, you'll need approx. 1oz of chocolate per cookie*

SALTY & SWEET SQUIRREL COOKIES

Squirrel = Nuts. This is maybe my one recipe that doesn't have chocolate or lemon in it, but it's one of my favourites. I love the combination of a little salt with my sweet, give it a whirl, I guarantee you will too! Be prepared, this recipe makes a bushel, can you make a bushel of cookies? Well a lot then, anywhere from 3 to 6 dozen, and believe you me, you'll be happy with your bushel.

142g of nuts – you choose which kind, but to keep with the theme, I suggest pecans, but it's really all about preference. Toast in a frying pan until they change color and you smell the nut, approx. 3-5 mins, set aside.
2/3 cup light brown sugar firmly packed
100g sugar
113g butter

92g coconut oil softened
2 tsp vanilla
¾ tsp butter-rum extract
1 tsp vinegar
1 egg
241g flour
½ tsp salt
1 tsp baking soda
227g butterscotch chips
67g sugar & 1 ¼ tsp salt for rolling

Preheat oven 375 degrees, line 2 cookie sheets with parchment & prepare your rolling mixture. Cream butter and coconut oil with the sugars until light in color. Add the egg until combined, then add the rest of the wet ingredients, beat until smooth. If it doesn't appear as creamy as you'd like, that just means your coconut oil wasn't softened enough, no worries my friend, we march on to the delight that awaits us! Add your dry ingredients a little at a time, until you have everything mixed in completely. I recommend the middle ice cream scoop, 4oz. However, it's your choice. Roll the dough into balls and roll in your sugar, salt mixture & place on the cookie sheet about an inch apart. Then press down gently. Bake **8 mins for the small cookie, 10 mins for med, 12 for large.**

- *As all my recipes, these freeze beautifully, & unless you're having a bake sale, you might want to do that for the late night snacking*
- *Now take a plate of these lip smacking cookies to the couch, put your feet up and be prepared for peace & serenity*

COCONUT CHUNK COOKIES

Like peanut butter and jelly, these two belong together. They NEED to be together, so lets make a date and show them a good time!

1 cup butter	2 ¼ cup flour
½ cup sugar	1 tsp baking soda
1½ cup brown sugar	1 tsp salt
2 eggs	2 cups chocolate chunks
½ tsp of vanilla	2 cups sweetened coconut

Preheat oven to 350 degrees and line you cookie sheet with parchment.

Cream butter and the sugars until light in color. Then add eggs & vanilla, beat until fluffy. Sift your dry ingredients & add a little at a time until combined. Using a 6oz ice cream, drop your balls onto your cookie sheet with room enough for them to spread and press down until they are the same thickness & even all around. Bake for **9 minutes.** Cool before consumption.

- *So as not to repeat myself, see the notes for Double Chunk Cookies. Do that.*

SHAME- LESS

*This section is all about **LESS**. Less sugar, less fat and generally less prep time. Some won't look like it, but trust that the average baked good has loads of sugar and fat, I fixed that. Here, you'll see mostly what I refer to as mini cakes, as in Muffins. You do not need a frosting to call it a cake, it just needs to be light, moist and delicious. But by all means, frost that muffin if that makes you sing.*

JUST TRY IT BROWNIES

1 (15.5 ounce) can black beans, rinsed and drained
3 eggs
4 tablespoons vegetable oil
1/4 cup cocoa powder
1 pinch salt
1 teaspoon vanilla extract

1/4 cup white sugar
1/2 cup of desired fruit, pineapple chunks, chopped strawberries, a fruit with substance
1/4 cup of shredded unsweetened coconut or chopped nuts (optional)

Preheat oven to 350 degrees. Lightly grease an 8x8 square baking dish.

In a blender or food processor puree black beans until smooth.

Add all ingredients EXCEPT the fruit and coconut or nuts until very smooth. Add the rest of ingredients just to combine, do not over blend or process.

Pour into pan and bake 25-30 minutes or until a toothpick inserted in the middle comes out clean

This recipe tends to be on the dry side, DO NOT OVERBAKE

When cool, sprinkle fruit and coconut or nuts on top and drizzle chocolate to "anchor" the toppings.

- *White chocolate is a nice contrast, and tastes delicious, melt 4oz of chocolate for drizzling with a spoon or fork and you'll forget this delight is made with black beans*

- *Normally a brownie can be left on the counter until it's devoured, but with a fresh fruit topping it's best to keep it in the fridge*

BRAN MINI CAKES

1 ½ cup of wheat bran – 100% Bran
Cereal works great
1 cup milk
½ cup of brown sugar
1/3 cup of veg oil
1 egg

½ tsp of van
1 cup of flour
1 tsp of baking soda
1 tsp of baking powder
½ tsp of salt
¾ cup of raisins

Preheat oven to 375 degrees, grease or line 12 muffin cups

Soak the bran in the milk, set aside. Cream together brown sugar with the veg oil, add egg & vanilla. Once combined, sift dry ingredients, add to the wet & mix until thoroughly combined. Fold in raisins. Drop by the method of preferred transfer…. 6oz ice cream scoop into your muffin cups and bake for **20 minutes.**

- *You can omit the raisins if that's not your fave, switch with chopped nuts or combine the two. Its all about that happy place*
- *If you like your muffins big & fat, make your muffin a 12oz, depends on how "less" it is you're going for*

RASPBERRY SWIRLY CHEESECAKE

*If I like chocolate and lemon for my sin-full desserts, raspberry is my jam for **Shame-Less** delights as they have a natural sugar while being a tart surprise to a rich cheesy delight such as this bad boy.*

Crust of Sir Graham X2 found in "**This and That**"
100g of raspberries
1 tsp of cornstarch
3 10oz (300g) low fat cream cheese – Softened

100g of sugar
3 eggs
2 tsp of vanilla
4 tblsp of flour

Preheat oven to 250 degrees and line a 9X13 rectangle pan with parchment.

Have your Sir Graham prepared & baked off. Heat raspberries on medium until broken & bubbly. If not using frozen berries add 1 tblsp of water, set aside. Beat cream cheese until smooth, if it remains lumpy, it needs to be softened further. Once smooth, add sugar again until smooth. Add the rest of the ingredients until thoroughly combined and smooth. Pour half the cheese mixture onto your crust & dollop the berry mixture on top, swirl by using a knife tip or a Chinese fork. Pour the rest of cheese mixture & repeat with berry mixture. Bake for **10 minutes,** lower heat to 110 degrees for **30 minutes,** then turn off oven, leave it in the oven for **1 hr.** Then with the door ajar, leave for another **1 hr.** Chill at room temperature for a minimum of **4 hrs.**

- *I quite often do this dessert at night, so that the last thing I do before bed is the last step, "with the door ajar" & just leave it in the oven overnight*

- *By all means, use any berry of your choice. I said raspberries are my jam, they certainly don't have to be yours, they should be, but like, your choice*

OAT & RAISIN COOKIES

*Who doesn't like Oatmeal Cookies? This is one of those recipes that when I tell people, I use very little sugar, it's not believed. That's because of the sugar packed raisins, so keep that in mind if you're cutting down on the calories. But lets be real, this isn't a cook book designed to lose a lot of weight, have you tried a cookie with **no** sugar? Don't.*

1 cup of butter	1 tsp of baking soda
¾ cup of brown sugar	3 tsp of cinnamon
2 eggs	½ tsp of salt
1 tsp of vanilla	3 cups of oats
1 ½ cups of flour	1 cup of raisins

Preheat oven to 350 degrees.

Cream your butter & sugar until the color becomes lighter, approx. 2 minutes, then add the eggs & vanilla until smooth. Sift the flour, soda, cinnamon & salt. Add a 1/3 at a time until well mixed, fold in the oats & raisins. Drop onto a non greased cookie sheet with a 6oz ice cream scoop, they will spread a little. Bake **12 minutes, OR** spread in a baking pan for bars, bake **25 minutes.**

- *I've mentioned this before, save time and double your recipe, they freeze great. Unless you have a Kyle in your life, then you won't need a freezer*

- *Use your baking ring so that your cookie is even all around, & if it's a large ring use two scoops, they spread less and there is nothing worse than crispy edges and raw middle*

PUMPKIN MINI CAKES

*This is one of those WOW muffins that tastes so good, you don't realize it is really **Less** in everything but the number of ingredients. Little known fact that pumpkin doesn't have any sugar and very little fat, so by my calculations, you can have more.*

2/3 cup of vegetable oil
½ cup of brown sugar
1 ½ cups of pumpkin
½ cup of un-sweetened applesauce
3 eggs
1 ½ tsp of vanilla
2 ½ cup of flour
½ cup of oats

4 tsp of pumpkin spice – see **"This & That"**
2 tsp of baking soda
1 tsp of baking powder
1 tsp of salt
¼ cup of raisins
2 tblsps each of butter, oats & flour mixed with a ¼ cup of brown sugar for topping - optional

Preheat oven to 350 degrees, line or grease your muffin cups. How many? Depends if you double the recipe as I always recommend that you use double the scoop to fill the cups.

Mix all your wet ingredients and add your sifted dry ingredients 1/3 at a time, except raisins, mixing thoroughly after each addition. Fold in raisins and using a 6oz ice cream scoop, drop 1 or 2 scoops into muffin tins and sprinkle with topping. Bake for **25 minutes** or until golden brown & toothpick comes out clean.

- *Just to be different, instead of raisins, chop 1 medium apple and fold that into the batter. Oh my, is apple & pumpkin a delicious twist*

APPLE CRUNCH COOKIES

This was a thought when the apples were falling off the tree and I already made a dozen pies and jams, something to freeze for the winter months or a lunch box treat, that was quick work of the juicy fruit.

1 ¼ cup of brown sugar
1 cup of butter
2 eggs
3 cups of flour
1 tsp of cinnamon
1 tsp of nutmeg
1 tsp of salt

1 tsp of baking soda
2 medium apples chopped
½ cup of chopped nuts – optional
5 tblsps each of butter, oats & flour mixed with ½ cup of brown sugar for topping

Preheat oven to 375 degrees, line your cookie sheet with parchment.

Beat brown sugar, butter & egg until light & fluffy. In a separate bowl mix the dry ingredients & add half at a time. Stir in apple & nuts. Drop onto cookie sheet, leaving space, as they spread, sprinkle with topping & bake **8 minutes for small cookies, 12 for large.**

- *This is where your cookie ring is very useful, it makes sprinkling the cookie with the topping easier. Not essential, but the topping is a little more even for a prettier cookie, for the 10 seconds they sit before they're eaten*

MONKEY MINI CAKES

What can I say? Yummy? Okay, yummy!

1/3 cup of vegetable oil
1/3 cup of sugar
1 egg
4 ripe bananas
1 ½ cup of flour

1 tsp of baking powder
1 tsp of baking soda
½ tsp of salt
¼ cup nuts - optional

Preheat oven to 350 degrees, line or grease your muffin cups. Again, the amount of cups depends if you double the recipe & double the scoop to fill the cups. Beat oil with sugar, banana & egg. Add half at a time, the sifted dry ingredients until incorporated. Fold in nuts & using a 6oz ice cream scoop, drop 1 or 2 scoops into muffin tins and sprinkle with topping. Bake for **25 minutes** or until golden brown & toothpick comes out clean.

- *That topping I'm so fond of, 2 tblsps each of butter, oats & flour with ¼ cup of brown sugar? Yeah, that one, use on these monkey treats if you want the added crunch. Do monkey's like crunch? Leaves yes, bananas yes, crunch…….hmmm*

WHITE CHOCOLATE & CRANBERRY COOKIES

It sounds odd, but surprisingly a terrific combo with the tart & sweet. The only thing to keep in mind with this weird cookie is, white chocolate has a higher sugar content. So maybe just eat one? Okay two, but then you'll be working out an extra 5 minutes, or was that 50? Oh just enjoy your cookie!

¾ cup of butter
½ cup of brown sugar
1 egg
2 tsp of vanilla
2 cups of flour

2 tsp of cornstarch
1 tsp of soda
½ tsp of salt
½ cup of white choc chips
¾ cup of frozen cranberries

Beat butter & sugar until light in color. Add egg & vanilla. Add sifted dry ingredients 1/3 at a time, beating after each addition until incorporated. Fold in chips & berries. **CHILL** 2 hrs or overnight.

Preheat oven to 350 degrees, line cookie sheet with parchment. Using a 6oz ice cream scoop to drop onto the cookie sheet & bake **10 minutes.**

- *Cookie ring, cookie ring, cookie ring*

RASPBERRY LEMON MINI CAKES

These are the best. That's it, that's all.

½ cup of vegetable oil
½ cup of sugar
1 cup of plain or Greek yogurt
2 eggs
1 tsp of vanilla
Juice & zest of one lemon

2 ¼ cups of flour
2 tsp of baking powder
½ tsp of baking soda
½ tsp of salt
1 ½ cups of raspberries

Preheat oven to 375 degrees & line muffin cups. Beat all the wet ingredients together until smooth. Sift dry ingredients together & add by 1/3 at a time until combined. Gently fold in raspberries or you might end up with pink batter, pink is a pretty color though. Bake **18 minutes** or until golden brown & a toothpick comes out clean.

- *I'll add 2 lemons if the berries are sweet or if I just want a really tart bite*
- *It doesn't matter if you are using fresh or frozen berries, the outcome is relatively the same. So it's entirely up to you*

THIS & THAT

BUTTERCREAM FROSTING

*This is the most versatile frosting I've come across, there isn't much you can't add to it for whatever you need it for & it works. This recipe is both **Sin-full & Shame-less,** because it adds a richness to your cakes & cupcakes, while using only a few ingredients.*

1 cup of butter - softened
4 cups of powdered sugar

2-3 tsp of extract

Cut the butter into cubes & cream in small amounts, until it's all combined. Cream for approx. 4-5 minutes. Add the powdered sugar a little at a time, approx. 2 minutes of beating in between each addition. When all incorporated it should be smooth & creamy, with no lumps, then add your extract. If you're baked goods are cool, frost away.

- *I just say "extract" because now you decide what flavor you want it. For example, when I make a lemon cake, I want just a plain frosting as in vanilla to counter the tart taste.*

- *The 2-3 tsps is how potent your extract is or how strong the flavor you want. For example, my vanilla extract is pure from Mexico, & it's incredibly potent, so 1 tsp is often enough.*

- *Taste, & taste again, until you've added the desired flavor. So only add a tsp at a time, you can add, but you can't take away, right?*

CRUST OF SIR GRAHAM

1 ½ cups of crushed graham crackers
¼ cup of sugar

1 tsp of cinnamon
6 tblsps of melted butter

Preheat oven to 375 degrees. Mix all ingredients together & stir until thoroughly incorporated. Press into a non-greased pan or individual ramekins, bake for **8 minutes.**

- *The only time I don't double this recipe is when I'm baking individual desserts. You get 4 to 8 individual bites, depending on the thickness of the crust & size of ramekins*

- *A single recipe is good for an 8X8 square cake pan, if you like a thinner crust*

- *Doubling the recipe for a 13X9 cake pan, or a thick crust for the 8X8*

- *My bulk section of my grocery store ran out of the crumbs, so instead of buying the box at twice the price, I used animal crackers & just zapped them in my food processor. Threw in some crushed almonds I had on hand from another baking day, & omitted the sugar. Which isn't necessary, but my butt is big enough, & it was a yummy change from the usual. You don't know unless you give it a whirl*

LEMON CURD

This is a great filling for cakes or just a topper on any dessert & you'll find yourself using it a lot. I've been known to have some in the fridge & smearing it on a cracker for a snack. Don't be shy, you know you want to.

½ cup of lemon juice
2 tsp of zest
¼ cup of sugar

3 egg yolks
6 tblsps of butter

In a medium sauce pan on medium low heat whisk together all of the ingredients until you get one bubble, then remove from the heat. Pour into a bowl or heat resistant container, cover with plastic wrap so it's touching the curd so there's no air, to prevent a crust from forming. Put it in the fridge to chill approx. 2 hours before using.

- *If you want this for a cake filling, depending on the layers, double this recipe & let cool completely before you spread onto your cake*

- *Left overs, if you have any, can be stored in the fridge up to 7 to 10 days*

GANACHE

I believe everyone who bakes should have a few things in their arsenal, such as Lemon Curd, Buttercream, Caramel & Ganache. With any of these 4, you have a topping or a smooth middle to an otherwise boring cake.

Chocolate

Heavy cream

Ganache is used for a glaze, a thick frosting, cake filling or truffles. It depends on your application of the ganache to the ratio of chocolate & cream. Chocolate is measured in weights, therefore the cream must be measured in weights as well. Regardless of what you want it for, the method remains the same. Heat the cream in a heavy sauce pan on medium heat only until it's vey warm, a slow simmer. Pour over the chocolate and let it sit for 3-4 minutes, stir until all the chocolate is melted & smooth. If you need a thinner ganache, add **warm** cream a little at a time to reach the consistency you are looking for. So now, how much ganache do I need to make my dessert pretty & delicious? There is no clear cut answer, it depends on how thick of a layer you enjoy on or in your masterpiece. But a good starting point is 10oz. It will decrease or increase with the more times you use this recipe & what for. It's a figure it out as you go & if you're like me, you will use this recipe a lot, for example, you only got half your cake frosted or only 15 truffles. That's when you will make your adjustments according to your preference. Either thinner frosting or smaller truffles, or increase the chocolate to fit your idea of perfect.

Cake filling = equal parts
Glaze = 1 part chocolate 2 part cream
Thin glaze = 1 part chocolate 2 part cream +

Truffles = 2 part chocolate 1 part cream

- *Any excess ganache can be left on your counter for 2 days, or become part of your fridge jungle up to a month. However, if your fridge is full of such things as last weeks dinners, you can clean out your fridge, but would rather not, you can freeze it also up to a month.*

- *If you would like a flavour added, by all means, let your freak fly in the amount of a 1 tsp at a time depending on your taste buds to the cream while heating.*

TRUFFLES

*What a beautiful gift these make, pick your recipients favorite flavor combo & you become **the** friend to have! Or if you're me, date night with my tv.*

10oz of chocolate
10oz of cream
1 tblsp of corn syrup

1 tsp of extract – optional
6oz of chocolate for dipping - optional

Follow the ganache instructions & chill for **2 hours**. Use a melon baller or spoon & roll into balls.

Now the fun begins, have your chocolate for dipping melted in a double boiler, which you can leave on the stove, but if you remove it, you might need to heat it up if it becomes too cool. Have your finely chopped nuts, pretzels, cocoa or sprinkles, basically anything that strikes your fancy, laid out. Once you've dipped your chocolate spheres in the melted chocolate, roll it in your desired topping & chill for **1 hour**.

- *If you're making this for Christmas gifts, lets say, freezing is a great option to doing everything the 23rd. Lay the truffles on a cookie sheet so they're not touching & freeze them for a minimum of **2 hours** before packaging them*

- *For a pretty & tasty alternative, dip the truffles in white chocolate and set them on a cookie sheet, then drizzle with dark chocolate, dip in dark, drizzle with white, you get the picture.*

- *This recipe is all about imagination, whatever flavor combo makes your heart skip a beat, is the perfect pairing*

GRANOLA BARS

These are the best hand held, on the go, slice of deliciousness that you absolutely do not feel guilty about consuming.

2 ½ cups of rolled oats
½ cup of chopped nuts of your choosing
¼ cup of honey
¼ cup of butter
1/3 cup of brown sugar

1 tsp of vanilla
¼ tsp of salt
¼ cup each of different add ins equalling up to ¾ cups. For example, ¼ cup of smarties, ¼ cup of coconut, ¼ cup of chocolate chips.

Preheat oven to 350 degrees, toast oats & nuts on a cookie sheet for **8 mins,** when all toasty, pour into a large bowl. Combine honey, butter & brown sugar in a saucepan on medium heat until the brown sugar is dissolved. Stir in vanilla & salt. If your add ins are chocolate, set aside for **15 minutes to slightly cool.** Pour over toasted oats & nuts and **thoroughly combine.** When each oat is touched by the honey mixture, pour into a 8X8 baking dish, press down & chill for an hour. Remove from the fridge, press the mixture down again, then chill for an additional hour. Cut into bars.

- *Lets talk about ad ins, if you want this energizing snack to be the ultimate in healthy, just keep your add ins to nuts or seeds*

- *Dried fruit is a perfect ad in, but they shouldn't be bigger than a raisin or your bar falls apart in your lap, then you'll be doing the 3 second rule & that defeats the purpose of "on the go" right?*

- *My favorite combination is, coconut, chocolate chips & almonds. But if the almonds hurt my wallet, I just double up on one or the other*

- *You can double the recipe and press into a 13X9 dish, but I recommend that you experiment first with the smaller dish & all your flavor combo's. That's how I found out that the bigger fruit pieces don't hold the honey "glue" enough, hence yogurt topping. Or you find out that pumpkin seeds really do not taste as yummy as you thought or you really dislike cranberries that aren't in a can. Are you picking up what I'm putting down?*

EGG – LESS

This is a substitute for eggs. If you get hives or you just need an egg & don't feel like running to the store for a dozen, this is a quick alternative.

Per one egg, combine
2 tblsps of water

1 tsp of vegetable oil
2 tsp of baking powder

- *Even if you have eggs, give this a try for all of your cakes, you'll be surprised at how moist your bite is*

PUMPKIN SPICE

An incredible handy spice to have for pies, mini cakes or hot toddy's on those less than warm days.

4 tsp of cinnamon
2 tsp of ginger
1 tsp of nutmeg

1 tsp of allspice
½ tsp of cloves

- *I am all about the homemade gifts, like putting this recipe in a pretty jar with a copy of the pumpkin mini cake recipe*
- *During the holidays, I triple this recipe & I often make it a few times during the season. As I said, a handy spice to have if you like to bake anything with pumpkin, and I can't help myself with pumpkin*

CARAMEL

Caramel is the most versatile topping, dipping or drizzling for any dessert.

2 cups of sugar
¼ cup of water
¾ cup of butter
1 cup of heavy cream

1 tsp of salt
For Salted Caramel
Omit the regular salt & add 1 tblsp of
sea salt

Combine all the ingredients in a heavy saucepan and stir to combine. Heat on medium high heat, stirring until it reaches a boil. Continue to cook **without stirring** until the mixture reaches an amber color. Swirl the pot Watch it carefully at this point, because the color changes rapidly & it burns quickly at this point. Remove from heat & cool for **15-20 minutes** before pouring into your jar or squeeze bottle. If you are using this for a spread or topping for a cake, cool an additional 2 hours.

THICK CARAMEL

Want a thick, gooey caramel? Then this is the one for you! Where as the Caramel Sauce drizzles & soaks into your cake, this Caramel sits on your layer of cake like a lovely sweet extra to your masterpiece.

½ cup of brown sugar	1 can of condensed milk
¼ cup of golden corn syrup	2 tsp of vanilla
¼ cup of butter	

Combine sugar, syrup & butter in a heavy in a heavy saucepan, stir to combine, then put down the spoon. Heat on medium heat until it boils then reduce the heat to low until it becomes the shade of amber you would like. Add the milk, stirring constantly until it becomes nice & thick, so for 5 mins. Add the vanilla & set aside to cool slightly before pouring into your desired container or tart shell. The same instructions as the regular caramel.

- It's quite alright to like your caramel thick. You don't have to conform to the thin drizzle if you don't feel like it. So enjoy this thick gooey loveliness anyway you want!

- Caramel apples? This is the sauce! Not saying, you can't use the thinner caramel, but this thick one works best. You however do NOT cool the sauce before you dunk your room temperature apple. Insert a popsicle stick into the end of any type of apple you like, then using the stick to hold, dunk the apple into the caramel. Let the excess run off & place it, stick up, onto a parchment lined baking sheet. Cool before consuming

Printed in the United States
By Bookmasters